Hitler Youth

Hitler Youth

The *Hitlerjugend* in War and Peace 1933–1945

BRENDA RALPH LEWIS

MBI Publishing Company

Library of Congress Cataloging-in-Publication Data available.

ISBN: 0-7603-0946-9

Editorial and design by
Amber Books Ltd
Bradley's Close
74-77 White Lion Street
London
N1 9PF

Project Editor: Charles Catton
Editor: Vanessa Unwin
Design: Floyd Sayers
Picture Research: TRH Pictures Ltd

Printed in Italy - Nuova GEP, Cremona

Picture credits
AKG: 6-7, 9, 13, 14, 15, 17, 18, 21, 30, 31, 33, 35, 37, 39, 41, 42, 44, 45, 46-47, 48, 49, 50, 52, 53, 62, 64-65, 66, 68, 70, 75, 76, 78, 80-81, 83, 84, 85, 86, 87, 88, 90, 91, 92, 94, 95, 96-97, 99, 101, 103, 104, 106, 107, 109, 110, 111, 112, 114-115, 116, 117, 119, 120, 122, 123, 124, 131, 136, 138, 158, 160, 161, 162, 166, 167, 168-169, 170, 173, 174, 178, 182. **Popperfoto**: 16, 20, 22, 23, 28-29, 32, 40, 54. **Robert Hunt Library**: 10-11, 59, 132-133, 135, 143, 177, 183. **TRH Pictures**: 8, 24, 25, 26, 36, 38, 57 (US National Archives), 58, 60, 61, 67, 69 (US National Archives), 72 (US National Archives), 73, 74 (US National Archives), 79 (US National Archives), 82 (US National Archives), 93 (US National Archives), 98 (US National Archives), 100 (US National Archives), 102 (US National Archives), 118 (US National Archives), 126, 127, 128, 129 (US National Archives), 134, 137, 139, 140, 142, 144, 145, 146, 147, 148, 150-151, 152, 153, 154, 156, 157, 163 (US National Archives), 164 (IWM), 172, 175 (US National Archives), 176 (US National Archives), 180 (US National Archives), 181, 184 (US National Archives), 185 (US National Archives), 186-187, 188 (US National Archives).

Contents

INTRODUCTION

The *Hitlerjugend* (the Hitler Youth), initially formed in 1922 by the nascent Nazi Party, promised young Germans excitement, achievement, comradeship, adventure and a great future in a great Germany. It was a potent message at a time when Germany, defeated in World War I only four years earlier and heavily punished by the victorious Allies, was a pariah among nations. The Hitler Youth gave young people what they were promised, but that was not its only purpose. What the Nazis meant to do was create a generation which knew nothing but Nazi principles and Nazi ideology, and to ensure that they reared their own children in exactly the same way.

The youth were vital to Adolf Hitler's purpose: to create a 'Thousand Year Reich' whose capital, Germania, would be the centre of the world. 'He alone who owns the youth gains the future', Hitler used to say, and he knew very well how he wanted the young to be prepared to carry on the torch across the centuries. He said in 1933:

I begin with the young. We older ones are used up. We are rotten to the marrow. We are cowardly and sentimental. We are bearing the burden of a humiliating past, and have in our blood the dull recollection of serfdom and servility. But my magnificent youngsters! Are there any finer ones in the world? Look at these young men and boys! What material! With them, I can make a new world. This is the heroic stage of youth. Out of it will come the creative man, the man-god .... When an

Left: Hitler salutes massed ranks of the
Marine Hitlerjugend, *the naval section of the*
Hitler Youth, *in 1938, accompanied by Baldur*
von Schirach, the Hitler Youth Leader.

opponent declares 'I will not come over to your side', I say calmly 'Your child belongs to us already ...What are you? You will pass on. Your descendants, however, now stand in the new camp. In a short time, they will know nothing but this new community.'

Nazification

The Nazification of the young began very early, at age six, but recruitment was selective and depended first of all on passing a test for racial, that is Aryan, 'purity'. The mystical Aryans, ostensibly from prehistoric India and Iran, were supposed by occultist philosophers like the Austrian Guido von List to be the sole founders of culture and civilisation. The Nordic or Germanic peoples – blond or dark blond, blue- or light brown-eyed, with the appropriate head shape – were presumed to be the most noble of all Aryans, so that, to be acceptable, recruits had to display their characteristics.

Their Aryan ancestry proven, entrants were admitted to the *Jungvolk*. Twelve years in the *Jungvolk* and the Hitler Youth accustomed them to spartan conditions, hard physical work, rigorous sports, ideological training and unthinking conformity to the Nazi ethos. Although this regime was uncompromising,

force was not the main weapon used to produce youth modelled along these lines. The Nazis understood what appealed to the young, most especially their yearning for importance, so often suppressed by older generations. They therefore set out to lure young Germans into the Hitler Youth through the boyish love of power displays – particularly sports and military-style parades – their natural fascination with weapons and uniforms, and the offer of outlets for male bonding and male aggression. Once netted, German youth was wide open to infusions of Nazi nationalism, militarism, racism, anti-semitism, the concept of superior and inferior races and the disposability of homosexuals, the mentally disabled and anyone else who did not fit the matrix of Aryan perfection.

Other youth organisations

Youth organisations as such were nothing new in Germany. By 1920, there were over 2000 groups and organisations, of which the most popular was the *Wandervogel*, formed in 1901. *Wandervogel* interest revolved around love of the countryside and the activities it afforded – hiking, skiing, camping – all later promoted in the Hitler Youth as healthy and appropriate for the builders of the Nazis' New Order.

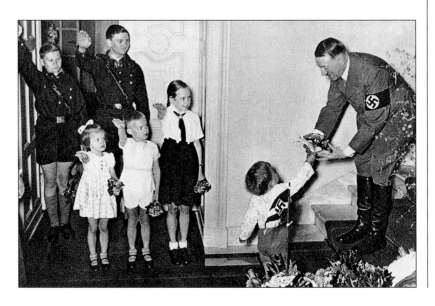

*Right: Adolf Hitler receiving flowers from a small boy whose shirt is decorated with the Nazi swastika. In the background three girls wait their turn, with two Hitler Youth behind them. In his book, **Inside the Third Reich**, Albert Speer asserted that Hitler had no idea how to treat children as individuals.*

The youth groups were often critical of the liberal Weimar government set up in Germany after World War I. Adolf Hitler had his own reasons for demonising the Weimar ministers as craven traitors who had accepted the Treaty of Versailles, which, in his view, made Germany little more than the creature of the victorious Allies. Consequently, since youthful idealists and Nazi fanatics appeared to have a hatred of the government in common, it seemed logical that thousands of young Germans would be ready and waiting to join when Hitler officially approved the establishment of the Hitler Youth on 27 July 1926. That, at least, was the theory.

In reality, the Hitler Youth first had to overcome the rival youth movements, some religious, some political, some social. This made recruitment a slow process, not solved to Nazi satisfaction until after Hitler took power as German Chancellor in 1933 and all non-Nazi youth movements, except for the Catholics, were banned.

When the Catholic associations were likewise forbidden in 1936, they carried on in secret, joining several other groups which operated underground. Some of them, such as the famous *Wiesse-Rose*, the White Rose students' movement centred around Munich University, actively campaigned against the Nazi regime. They suffered brutal suppression, long terms in prison or the concentration camps and, for the most stubbornly resistant, the death sentence.

Hitler Youth wrongdoing

The Hitler Youth itself was by no means lily-white, despite the dazzling image created by Nazi propaganda and the dramatic shows of youth solidarity displayed at the Nuremberg and other rallies. Within both the *Jungvolk* and the Hitler Youth, all manner of crimes were committed. Rules were broken, discipline defied, moral imperatives (especially those dealing with homosexuality) were ignored and the movement acquired a reputation, never officially admitted, for brutality, decadence and evil influence.

Above: Captured by the Americans, on 23 March 1945, at Frankenthal in Rheinland-Pfalz, this member of the Volkssturm – *the 'People's Army' – is frisked for weapons.*

Nevertheless, whether they abused it, defied it or embraced it, Nazi rule in Germany meant ultimate catastrophe for a whole generation of young Germans. Thousands who joined the *Hitlerjugend* Division that was formed in 1943 were killed on the frontline. Thousands more died in the *Volkssturm*, the People's Militia formed in 1944. More died in guerrilla attacks on Allied troops as they rolled inexorably into Germany and closed in for the kill on the 'Thousand Year Reich' in 1945.

When Nazi Germany finally surrendered on 7 May 1945, 19 years of the Hitler Youth came to an end. The defiance of those who resisted in movements like the *Weisse-Rose*, shortened their lives or left them scarred by nightmare experiences at the hands of Nazi interrogators. Others, transformed in the Hitler Youth into model Nazis, found they had been led to believe in dreams of greatness that never came true, and to expect a glorious future which turned instead to the dust of total disaster.

CHAPTER 1

BEGINNINGS

On 19 March 1922, an invitation to German youth appeared in the *Völkischer Beobachter*, the newspaper of the *National-sozialistische Deutsche Partei* (NSDAP, also known as the Nazi Party):

We demand that the Nationalist Socialist Youth, and all other young Germans, irrespective of class or occupation, between 14 and 18 years of age, whose hearts are affected by the suffering and hardships afflicting the Fatherland, and who later desire to join the ranks of the fighters against the Jewish enemy, the sole originator of our present shame and suffering, enter the Youth League of the NSDAP ...

No subscription would be charged and all that was required of potential recruits was 'love of one's country and people, enjoyment of honest open combat and of healthy physical activity, the veneration of ethical and spiritual values, and the rejection of those values originating from Jewry ...'

With the violent language that would soon become customary for their pronouncements, this statement set out the fundamentals that fuelled the Nazi purpose. Firstly, there was fury at the fate of defeated Germany, once a mighty military and imperial power, but now, after losing World War I, a remnant of her former self. Burdened with war guilt and reparations, her colonies confiscated and her armed forces dwindled to impotence, Germany had also suffered the loss of 13 per cent of her territory

Left: Flag bearers of the Hitler Youth march past enthusiastic crowds to honour Admiral Adolf von Trotha at a commemoration of the anniversary of the Battle of Jutland in 1916.

in Europe to new neighbouring countries such as Poland and Czechoslovakia. Secondly there was the atavistic hatred of the Jews who, the Nazis believed, had conspired with their other great enemy, the Communists, to engineer the 'great betrayal' which ended World War I: the Treaty of Versailles. It was this treaty, signed in 1919 by the Nazis' third most hated body, the Weimar government of inter-war Germany, that Adolf Hitler had personally sworn to overturn.

Hitler's rise

After the World War I, Hitler joined the propaganda unit of a volunteer corps made up of army veterans. His job was to spy on political meetings and bookmark the liberal, socialist and other left-wing organisations so detested by military and other right-wing groups. One organisation examined by Hitler in 1919 was the seemingly innocuous German Workers' Party which came under suspicion because of the second word in its title. In investigating the German Workers' Party, Hitler saw an excellent opportunity. Gradually he infiltrated the Party, took it over, renamed it *Nationalsozialistische Deutsche Partei* (NSDAP), and transformed it into an organisation with an extremely ambitious agenda. This was to restore Germany to its former greatness, turn her into a power which other nations would fear and respect, and punish the 'November criminals' whose signatures on the Versailles Treaty had brought the Fatherland so low.

German youth was to play a significant part in Hitler's grand design. He envisaged them leading the Nazi spearhead into a glorious future brought about by the dawn of the 'Aryan millennium'. Initially, the idea of youth participation came from Gustav Adolf Lenk, a young man who polished pianos for a living. After hearing Hitler speak at open-air meetings in Munich, Lenk became a keen devotee of National Socialism. At the end of 1921, he applied to join the Party, only to be told that, at 17, he was not old enough. Unabashed, Lenk enquired whether he could join the Party's youth section. There was no youth section, but it was suggested that he create one.

At first, there was some opposition from within the Party. Nazis like Adolf Drexler, one of the founder members, believed that since the Party was itself so new, consolidation should take precedence over expansion. However, Hitler approved of Lenk's idea and pulled rank on all of them. He talked Drexler round, sent a circular informing all Party members that a youth section was to be set up and followed it up with the invitation which appeared in the *Völkischer Beobachter*.

A problem immediately made itself apparent. Numerous, well-established rivals were already on the scene, which doubtless explained why the initial response to the Nazi Youth League was so paltry. On 13 May 1922, the Nazi Party hired a large Munich beer hall, the Bürgerbräu Keller, for a public meeting at which the official founding of the Youth League would be announced. A large number of people turned up and crowded into the beer hall to hear speeches by Hitler, the leader of the *Sturmabteilung* (the SA, or Nazi storm-troopers) Johann Ulrich Lintzch, and Gustav Lenk. However, there were only 17 youths among them.

The German Youth League

Lenk was nevertheless formally appointed Youth League leader and immediately began organising. Within a short time, he announced that the Youth League would consist of two sections which were forerunners of the later *Jungvolk* and Hitler Youth. The younger section, the *Jungsturm* Adolf Hitler, was for 14 to 16 year olds, and the senior section was for youths aged 16 to 18. Though still only 18, not especially charismatic and, compared to Hitler, no public speaker, Lenk was dynamic, innovative and endlessly energetic. He had to be, considering the formidable challenge presented by his rivals who had several years' seniority among their credentials. In 1913, German youth movements were so far developed that 13 federations – including the *Wandervögel* (Birds of Passage) founded in

1896 and the Pathfinder Boy Scouts of 1908 – were represented at the celebrations for the twenty-fifth anniversary of Kaiser Wilhelm II's accession to the throne. On 12 October 1913, a year before the outbreak of World War I, Free German Youth Day saw a parade of upright young men – every one abstainers from alcohol and cigarettes – who were devoted, like the putative Nazi Youth League, to healthy, outdoor, back-to-nature activities.

Strong competition

The Nazis were therefore offering little that was new, and did not aim to cater for other interests already well covered by more specialist organisations. For instance, the Evangelist youth movement which had originated in 1883, and the Catholic youth movement of 1909, took care of the youth's spiritual side. The Germania federation was one of two concentrating on abstinence, while the workers' socialist movement, founded in

1903 was, by its very nature, the political opposite of the hard-right Nazis.

Lenk nevertheless persisted and gradually, units of the Youth League were established in Nuremberg, Zeitz, Dresden, Hanau and Dortmund. Outside Germany, Lenk managed to plant the flag of the Youth League among the Sudeten Germans in Czechoslovakia and also in Austria, where he had contacts with the Nazi Party in Vienna. On 28 January 1923, the *Jungsturm* Adolf Hitler made its appearance at the first Nazi *Parteitag* (party day), a precursor to the later Nuremberg rallies.

There, the boys were solemnly presented with special pennants which featured the Nazi Party's swastika symbol on a white background, an early instance of the dramatic

Below: Hitler's failed putsch of 9 November 1923. This picture shows a lorry-load of uniformed 'shock' troops, including some youths, in a street in Munich.

pageantry which was to be so dominant in Nazi stagecraft.

All the same, despite the public show, the growth of new units and a promotion for Lenk as 'national' rather than 'regional' leader, the Youth League was still a relatively minor organisation. This became apparent in May 1923 when Lenk thought he was in a position to publish a special youth magazine, the *Nationale Jungsturm*. Subscribers proved to be too few and the magazine failed. Renamed the *Nationalisozialistiche Jugend*, it ended up as a supplement to the *Völkischer Beobachter*.

Below: Pre-war Germany offered many opportunities for organised youth activities. The **Wandervögel**, *founded in 1896, stressed the attractions of the countryside.*

This was an embarrassing setback for Lenk. However, he had pushed back frontiers that still eluded the Nazi Party as a whole. In 1920 and 1921, attempts had been made to fuse the Party in Munich, its centre in Germany, with like-minded groups in Hanover, Czecho-slovakia and Upper Silesia in Poland. These attempts had foundered because these groups refused to accept Hitler's terms that they accept him as sole leader. The situation was no different two years later in 1923, but with 55,000 members, the Nazi Party had outpaced all the other organisations in Munich. The Bavarian capital was a political hotbed, seething with opposition to the Weimar government. Among the right-wing groups, the Nazis were therefore in pole position to take advantage of the hatred felt towards Weimar

ministers and their acceptance of the Versailles Treaty. Unrest from both the political right and left had produced an atmosphere of chaos, barely kept under control by troops. The fragile balance of Germany was put in even greater doubt by the desperate financial crisis which occurred in June 1923 when the German Mark collapsed under the weight of reparations payments, and inflation began to run riot through the economy.

The French occupation of the Ruhr in January 1923 and their subsequent seizure of coal, timber and other materials as reparations in kind had provoked strikes, street demonstrations and sabotage, and so set a perfect scene for the Nazi Party's first rally. On 27 January, flags, banners, pennants and the Aryan swastika emblem – since 1920 the symbol of the Nazi Party – plastered the streets of Munich as, to vociferous applause, Hitler raged against the Treaty of Versailles, and the Weimar government and all its works.

The Munich putsch

The reception he received seems to have persuaded him that the time had come for a putsch. This was intended to be Hitler's bid for power which would begin with the kidnapping of Bavarian government leaders. On 9 November 1923, the fourth anniversary of the proclamation of the Weimar Republic, Hitler marched 3000 Nazis to the Bürgerbräu Keller and invaded a political meeting held by the Bavarian state commissioner, Gustav von Kahr. Hitler leapt onto a chair, brandishing a pistol. He fired a shot into the ceiling and proclaimed: 'The National Revolution has begun!'

But there was no revolution. The Bavarian police intervened and Hitler was forced to escape to avoid arrest. The authorities caught up with him two days later, and on 1 April 1924, after a five-week trial, Hitler and other leading Nazis were sentenced to imprisonment. Hitler received a five year sentence, though he was released on parole after only eight months. Both the Nazi Party and the Youth League were disbanded and outlawed on Weimar government orders.

Above: Dressed somewhat self-consciously in his rural outfit, cap at a jaunty, casual angle, this member of the **Wandervögel** *poses for the camera with the organisation's banner.*

However, those who believed that this was the end of Adolf Hitler had not been listening properly at his trial. He had used the dock like a podium, boldly peddling his Nazi message and asserting that Germany and the whole world would one day come round to his way of thinking. His performance made him better known in Germany than he had been before the attempted putsch, for which he was proud to claim sole credit.

Lenk's continued efforts

Meanwhile, Gustav Lenk twice attempted to re-found a youth movement under innocent-sounding names: the Patriotic Youth Association of Greater Germany or the Greater German Youth Movement. The Bavarian authorities guessed that these were simply covers for the Nazi Youth League, and Lenk joined Adolf Hitler and the other Nazi leaders

Above: Boys and girls – and their marching drums – take a rest while hiking in the countryside. The two girls closest to the camera are not ideally shod.

in Landsberg fortress. Hitler was released on 1 December 1924, and Lenk at about the same time.

Although Hitler had entered Landsberg as a failed fanatic, just another extremist with strange political ideas, he came out in much more dangerous guise: as a man who realised why his putsch had gone wrong, and how he could get it right next time. State Prosecutor Stenglein had more or less told him how in his closing speech at the trial. 'It is understandable that the enthusiastic youth suffers from impatience', Stenglein told the court, 'but youth must be disciplined and led in the right direction by mature men. Impatience must be replaced by the ability to work quietly and confidently for the future, waiting with clenched teeth until the hour is ripe.'

With this blueprint for the future in mind, Hitler had come to realise that power should not be seized by the throat, but won at the polls: the Nazi Party would in future participate in the democratic process and then pervert it to its own purposes.

Mein Kampf

Hitler had set out those purposes while in Landsberg fortress. There, with the assistance of his devoted henchman Rudolf Hess, he wrote his semi-autobiography, *Mein Kampf* (My Struggle) a turgid, often misspelt, agglomeration of crude prejudice, conspiracy theory, race hatred and perverted Darwinism. Nevertheless, *Mein Kampf*, which became a bestseller after publication in 1925 and made

Hitler a rich man, set out very clearly the sequence of conquest, subjection and exploitation that was going to take place in World War II.

Hitler was no sooner out of prison than he announced his intention of rebuilding the Nazi Party with himself as leader. He issued an invitation to all German nationalists to join him. The Youth League, too, was revived, but not with Lenk at its head. Lenk had disgraced himself by showing independent tendencies: he even suggested that Hitler was not capable of absolute, undisputed leadership. Lenk soon paid for his temerity. A whispering campaign labelled him a traitor who had had his hand in the till. The rumours had the desired effect: Lenk lost control of the youth movement.

Gruber takes over

His place was taken by one of his own group leaders, Kurt Gruber, a law student who had joined the Nazi Party in 1923. Aged 21, Gruber fitted the 'youth leading youth' pattern thought most likely to attract potential members to what was now known as the Greater German Youth Movement. Gruber first came to Hitler's attention in 1927 at the Nuremberg Rally of 1927, when he led a group of 300 boys in a march-past. Hitler was also impressed by Gruber's organisational skills and by his new ideas. Concentrating on the mass of working-class urban youth, Gruber increased the size of the youth movement tenfold between 1927 and 1928, his first two years, and generated another 30 per cent increase between 1928 and 1929. He introduced uniforms based on those worn by the *Sturmabteilung* (the SA, also known as

Below: Berlin members of the Pathfinders parade with their flags in 1932. Their religious connections are evident in the crosses on their banners.

Brownshirts). Members of the Greater German Youth Movement would wear the same brown shirts and black shorts, together with a special armband featuring the Nazi swastika with a horizontal white stripe: this differentiated them from the SA, whose armband carried a white circle as background to the swastika. Gruber also introduced departments into the Hitler Youth, emulating the organisation within the main party. Among the 14 sections of the Hitler Youth thus established were those covering sport, press and propaganda and education and culture.

This was all part of the Nazi infrastructure Hitler was preparing to install as and when he took power. Power, however, seemed far off at that time and Hitler was astute enough to realise that he would have to be patient. The atmosphere in Germany was much more stable than it had been in the firework days of 1923, and therefore far less conducive to violent revolution. This was largely the work of Gustav

Left: At the Nazi Party Rally in Nuremberg in 1929, a time when the Nazi Party was beginning to expand rapidly, Hitler grasps the Blutfahne *or 'Blood Banner', supposedly stained with the blood of the Nazis who died in the failed Munich putsch in 1923. An inspirational symbol for the Nazis, the 'Blood Banner' was ceremonially touched by all flags at this and later rallies. Hitler Youth banners were no exception, and members of the organisation were taught to revere the early martyrs of the Nazi Party.*

Stresemann, Foreign Minister in the Weimar Republic, who was working to restore Germany to international respectability and to forge a reconciliation with France. The currency crisis and subsequent inflation were brought under control through a 200-million dollar loan from the United States, agreed under the Dawes Plan of 1924. A more feasible arrangement for the payment of reparations was made in London, the location towards the end of 1924 of the signing of a commercial treaty between Britain and Germany.

Versailles confirmed

On 16 October 1925 at Locarno in Switzerland a treaty was signed which confirmed arrangements imposed at Versailles in 1919. Germany's frontiers with France and Belgium were restated and other treaties of mutual guarantee and arbitration to settle disputes were made with Belgium, Czechoslovakia and Poland. The inviolability of the demilitarised Rhineland was established at the same time. This later led to the withdrawal of British and French troops in 1930, five years earlier than the maximum period of occupation laid down at Versailles. The first result of Locarno transpired the following year. On 8 September 1926, Germany was admitted into the League of Nations, a sure sign that respectability had been regained.

All this meant that the Nazi Party had lost much of its sting. Hitler nevertheless used this calm after the storm to gainful effect, most significantly in rebuilding the Nazi Party and consolidating his undisputed leadership. On 27 February 1925, there was a rare occasion when he let the mask slip and the fires of his fanaticism blaze. On his return to the Munich beer hall where his putsch had taken place two years before, Hitler harangued an audience of about 4000 for two hours, pouring forth all his venomous hatred of Jews, communists and the Weimar government. The Bavarian authorities took prompt action and banned Hitler from speaking in public. The ban was not lifted for two years, though the Nazi Party itself was no longer proscribed and the *Völkischer*

Beobachter had been allowed to resume publication. Prussia, too, had forbidden Hitler to make public speeches, so taking away his most powerful political weapon and the lynchpin of his success so far.

Now that Hitler was silenced, it was presumed that he could do no more damage, but this was a mistaken idea. The background which he now occupied was just the place for Hitler to make his preparations. Out of the public eye, but by no means out of action, Hitler worked tirelessly to recruit more and more members to the Nazi Party, and though progress was only gradual, numbers rose from 27,000 in 1925 to 49,000 in 1926 and by 1929, to 178,000. In 1930, membership stood at 210,000.

Over this same period, the Greater German Youth Organisation was regaining its place in the Nazi scheme of things. By 1926, when some of its members took part in the two-day rally held in the city of Weimar on 3 and 4 July, a major advance in its status was imminent. Ironically enough, at that juncture, Weimar was one of the few places in Germany where Hitler was permitted to make speeches.

Kurt Gruber's great moment came on Sunday 4 July. That day, youth leaders and Nazi Party officials convened and officially changed the name of the movement to *Hitler Jugend, Bund der Deutschen Arbeiterjugend* (Hitler Youth), which became part of the SA. Gruber was proclaimed first *Reichsführer* and was also appointed youth adviser to the directorate of the Nazi Party. Three weeks later, on 2 July, Hitler gave his official recognition to the Hitler Youth, whose symbol was to be the magical Nordic rune of the Sun and Victory.

The showmanship inherent in this and later public appearances was an effective part of the blatant, but cleverly conceived, Nazi propaganda machine. The public face of the Party and the Hitler Youth was deliberately used to impress Germans as a whole with Nazi zeal and vigour. Music and rhythm were integral to this display of strength and resolve.

The first substantial public performance by the Hitler Youth took place on 19 and 20 August 1927, when 300 youth, proudly led by

Above: The 'Adolf Hitler March', in which dedicated Hitler Youth walked great distances to the rallies. These Youth are marching from Berlin to Nuremberg in 1935.

Gruber, marched with 30,000 Brownshirts at the Nuremberg Rally. This was the second Nazi *Parteitag* in a series that later came to typify aggressive Nazi jingoism. They featured fiery, near-hysterical speeches by Hitler, Goebbels and other Nazi leaders, all delivered against a backdrop of theatrical pageantry and symbolism. The first *Parteitag* had taken place in 1923 and, like the 1927 event, was a relatively small affair. The first grand-scale Nuremburg Rally was staged in 1929, when Hitler took the salute as 2000 Hitler Youth goose-stepped past and a vast crowd noisily applauded. Some 400 of the boys had walked from Berlin to Nuremberg, so establishing the tradition of the 'Adolf Hitler March', which was afterwards used to typify youthful hardiness and devotion to the Party. Thunderous, imposing Wagner overtures were played and martial songs were sung. There was a torchlight procession, a fireworks display and bonfires. The surrounding buildings were awash with swastika flags and Nazi insignia. It was all designed to stir the emotions and to characterise the power and might of the Nazi Party and its undisputed Führer.

A great deal of this was still considered hot air in 1927 and 1929. The Nazis were not nearly as almighty as the melodrama of the *Parteitage* portrayed them. In 1924, for instance, the Nazis

Right: Marching for National Socialism. Hitler Youth marching to a weekend camp where they would do hard physical exercise and weapons training.

took part in two national elections for the Reichstag, the German legislature, but won only 32 seats in the first and 14 seats in the second. In 1928, their share of the vote had declined: they won only 12 seats. Nevertheless, preparations were being made behind the scenes that would one day change this modest scenario. Support was successfully canvassed from the rich and powerful, such as the major German industrialists, and from the discontented, such as ex-army officers or students. On 28 September 1928, Hitler's personal position was improved when Prussia followed Bavaria's example of 1927 and lifted the ban on his speeches.

Growth of the Hitler Youth

Meanwhile the Hitler Youth continued to develop and grow in scope. Contacts were made with young Germans in the Sudetenland of Czechoslovakia and in Poland, where they had been parted from the Fatherland by the Treaty of Versailles. Within Germany, the Hitler Youth increased its catchment area by the creation of a special organisation for boys aged 6 to 10, who had to pass tests in athletics, the rigours of outdoor camping, racial awareness and history as rewritten by the Nazi Party. The next stage, the *Jungvolk*, was created to further the Nazi education of boys from age 10 until they graduated at the age of 14 into the Hitler Youth proper.

On 18 November 1928, the diligent Kurt Gruber introduced the first *Reichsappell*, a junior version of the *Parteitag* or 'Party Day'. It required the Hitler Youth to assemble at public rallies on several days each year to receive orders and hear the latest Nazi proclamations. However, the *Reichsappell* was much more than a big public show. The Nazi Party believed that the Jews, among other 'powers', possessed a monopoly of the news, and the *Reichsappell* was one way of ensuring that the

Left: A Hitler Youth proudly poses for his portrait in full uniform. Both before and during the war, the Hitler Youth seemed to exert an inexorable pull on the young.

Above: When books by Jewish and liberal authors were burned on 27 March 1933, Nazi uniforms as worn by the Hitler Youth were very much in evidence.

Youth received the 'right', Nazi, message. Another was the setting up of a special Hitler Youth news service and the publication of youth newspapers. By these means, the Nazi Party aimed to ensure that 'young, social revolutionary-minded Germans', as Gruber termed them, were aware of nothing beyond the 'information' it wanted them to absorb.

Baldur von Schirach

Inevitably, though, Gruber's attainments and the favour he enjoyed from Hitler roused envy and competition from other Nazis, who saw the Hitler Youth as a useful platform for their own advancement. The rot set in for Gruber in 1928, when the ambitious Baldur von Schirach was appointed Leader of the Nazi Student Association and adviser for youth affairs at Nazi Party headquarters in Munich. As Gruber soon discovered, von Schirach, who had joined the Party in 1925, was a difficult act to match. He had all the obvious advantages that came from a favoured upbringing as the son of a wealthy Prussian ex-army officer and theatre director and an American mother whose ancestry went back as far as, ironically, two signatories of the American Declaration of Independence.

Above: Members of a Hitler Youth rally give the Nazi salute on 1 May 1933. The rallies would subsequently grow in size and spectacle as the membership expanded.

Von Schirach combined fresh-faced good looks with a top-class education and came fully fledged with the 'correct' Nazi views, which included anti-semitism and, curiously, a hatred for his own aristocratic class. Another useful asset was the silver tongue, well-oiled with the flattery which the Führer found irresistible. Von Schirach was not the only prominent Nazi to discover this convenient truth, but he was better at it than anyone else. He was, in fact, the ultimate fan: he fantasised over Hitler, wrote romantic poems about him and described him as 'this genius grazing the stars'. 'Loyalty', von Schirach declared 'is everything, and everything is the love of Adolf Hitler.'

Unsurprisingly, von Schirach was widely suspected of being homosexual.

Hitler could hardly help noticing this likely youth, and was gratified to find that his rich, well established family offered him their friendship and support. The von Schirachs became Hitler's confidantes and frequently entertained him in their luxurious home. In return, the Führer advanced and encouraged their son, prompting him to study at Munich University, where von Schirach read German folklore and art history. After graduating, he joined the SA, where he learned the techniques of violent thuggery which the Brownshirts used on the Nazis' opponents.

Struggle for control

Gruber fought a rearguard action to fend off von Schirach by appealing to the Hitler Youth for their undivided loyalty, and establishing two more newspapers, *Die Junge Front* (The Young Front) and *Hitlerjugend Zeitung* (The Hitler Youth Newspaper). Unfortunately for Gruber, neither was a success. For the moment, though, he managed to retain the upper hand and was bolstered by the announcement in April 1929 that the Hitler Youth was the one and only official youth movement of the Nazi Party. The statistics seemed encouraging, even though they represented only 0.3 per cent of the 4.3 million youth in Germany at that time. In 1926, when the Hitler Youth received official sanction from the Führer, the movement had comprised 80 branches with 700 members. By 1929, the figures had risen to 13,000 members and 450 branches, a substantial rise.

The Great Depression

By this time, the Hitler Youth, like the Nazi Party itself, was about to experience an unprecedented upsurge in popularity with the cardinal event of 1929: the collapse of the Stock Market on New York's Wall Street on 29 October. With that, a miasma of slump, depression, bankruptcy, poverty and hopelessness blanketed the world and, in Germany, brought to an abrupt end the fragile stability the Weimar government had built up over the previous four years. For the Nazis, this was the perfect opportunity. A shocked, despairing electorate, robbed of savings, investments, employment and, in some cases, homes, a government destabilised, widespread economic ruin, a near-worthless national currency – this was just the sort of catastrophe that prompted the frightened and the dispossessed to call for strong-arm action. And there was the Nazi Party with its omnipotent leader, its militarised cadres, its aggressive nationalism and its devoted youth, ready to administer the simple, drastic solutions which democracy, with its free, consensual nature, could never contemplate.

All the same, democracy still had sufficient teeth to crack down on the Nazi Party. A Hitler Youth rally in Berlin on 20 March 1930 resulted in swift police action. The rally, under the title of 'From Resistance to Attack', featured provocative, rabble-rousing speeches from Goebbels, the Nazi *gauleiter* (governor) of Berlin, and from Karl Gruber. As a result, the authorities banned propaganda marches and forbade young Germans from joining the Hitler Youth on pain of fines or expulsion from school. In response, the Hitler Youth gave themselves innocuous names like 'Friends of Nature'. This fooled no one, and it seems likely that the Hitler Youth became all the more attractive for being forbidden.

A tussle of the generations ensued. Parents, many of whom had never wanted their children to associate with the Hitler Youth,

Below: An autograph for a dedicated fan of the Führer. Hitler Youth members were encouraged to idolise Adolf Hitler, despite his being very different from the 'Aryan ideal'.

attempted to use the ban to strengthen their own case. They were not always successful. The major youth organisation run by the Catholic Church actively prevented their own young people from joining. To keep them within their own fold, the Church emulated the Hitler Youth by introducing activities it had formerly shunned, like rifle shooting. The drain nevertheless continued, swelling the ranks of the Hitler Youth with new recruits who delighted in the martial marches and rallies which were specifically designed to inspire and excite them.

Below: Hitler Youth march through Nuremberg in 1933, saluted by Baldur von Schirach. Also visible is Streicher, founder of the anti-Semitic newspaper, **Der Stürmer.**

All Quiet on the Western Front

The greatest coup achieved by the Hitler Youth at this time was the disruption and ultimate cancellation of the anti-war film, *Im Westen nichts neues* (known in English as *All Quiet on the Western Front*). The original novel, published in 1929, was the work of the German writer Erich Maria Remarque, whose experiences in the trenches in World War I had turned him into a pacifist. His novel told the adventures of a young boy who joined the army full of patriotism and excitement, only to become disillusioned when confronted by the horrors of modern mechanised warfare. An international bestseller – reflecting the disgust with war which was a common emotion worldwide after 1918 – *All Quiet on the Western Front* was filmed in Hollywood in

1930 and emulated the book's success by winning the Oscar for Best Picture in 1931.

In both Austria and Germany, however, it met with furious opposition. Remarque's novel was banned in Austria on 18 August 1929, and when the film was shown in Vienna, the performance was seriously disrupted by a group of Hitler Youth demonstrating inside the cinema. The same thing happened in several German cities, where the Youth caused so much trouble that showings were cancelled and the film was ultimately withdrawn by the distribution company.

Electoral success

Meanwhile Hitler maintained his resolve to gain power in Germany by democratic means and the Hitler Youth was active in campaigning for the Nazis in the national election set for 14 September 1930. Church, family and all other opposition to the Nazis and the Hitler Youth received a severe setback that day: the Party polled 6,409,000 votes, nearly eight times their 1928 showing. This support earned the Nazis 107 seats in the Reichstag, making them the second largest party in the legislature.

By this time, Karl Gruber's position as Hitler Youth leader was rapidly weakening. In 1931, he had two rivals angling to unseat him: not only Baldur von Schirach, but also Ernst Röhm, who had been recalled from Bolivia by Hitler to reorganise the SA and get rid of its rebellious elements. Röhm, a homosexual adventurer, was much more brutish than the upper-class von Schirach, and he and Hitler had known each other for a long time. In fact, it was Röhm, then an army captain, who recruited the former Corporal Hitler to investigate the German Workers' Party in 1919. The SA originated from various units of the disbanded German Army which Röhm had kept together in different guises during the interwar years, and it was placed at Hitler's disposal in 1921. Two years later, Röhm took part in Hitler's failed Putsch. He was briefly imprisoned and expelled from the German army. Afterwards, he went to Bolivia, where he worked as a military instructor.

Hitler was aware that Röhm's radical ideas alarmed the landowners and industrialists he was diligently drawing into the Nazi Party as a source of funds. For the moment, though, Hitler had a use both for Röhm and his brute-force tactics: the task of cleaning up and bringing the SA under control. That done, Hitler declared himself head of the SA, with Röhm as his Chief of Staff. Röhm's return, however, meant collision with Kurt Gruber, since the Hitler Youth was still a department of the SA. Gruber was soon made to feel the heat when Hitler placed him as Röhm's subordinate, at Röhm's request.

Now that Gruber was being ousted, Baldur von Schirach weighed in to kick him further down. Hitler Youth publications, which Gruber had pioneered, were suffering sales and circulation problems due to local bans on the organisation. Fundraising was also faltering. Von Schirach claimed that he could reverse this trend and revitalise the Hitler Youth, and also accused Gruber of poor organisational skills. At one time, this would have been patently untrue. However, Gruber was losing his touch. The Hitler Youth had become sloppy. Reports from district leaders came in late and were carelessly written. There were delays in getting the subscription money to Nazi headquarters. Von Schirach was not alone in his anti-Gruber campaign. Ernst Röhm struck further blows by criticising Gruber for the low membership numbers in the Hitler Youth.

Gruber's fall

Kurt Gruber was now a desperate man. He promised Hitler the impossible: a doubling of the Hitler Youth membership within a year. This was all to no avail. In October 1931, Nazi Party headquarters in Munich announced that Gruber's resignation had been accepted, even though Gruber had not offered to resign. Nevertheless, outmanoeuvred and slandered by his rivals, let down by his subordinates, Gruber's three-year tenure of leadership came to an ignominious end, and before October was out, Baldur von Schirach had taken possession of the Hitler Youth.

CHAPTER 2

ORGANISING THE YOUTH

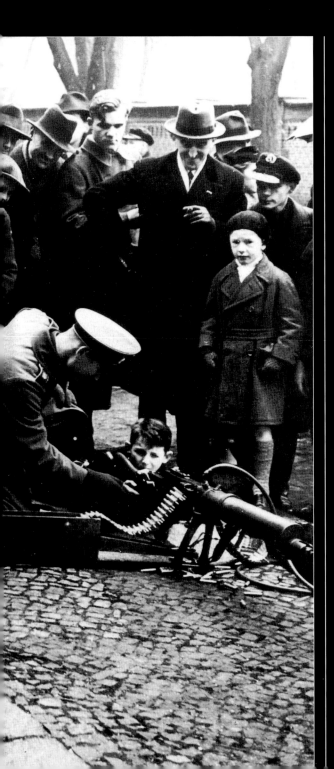

On the face of it, Baldur von Schirach, with his boyish looks, plump physique and effeminate manners, was the last man suited to lead the toughs of the Hitler Youth, many of whom came from working-class backgrounds. Von Schirach, by contrast, was an aristocrat who had grown up in a much more refined atmosphere, where the emphasis was on music, literature, theatre and poetry. These cultural interests were the antithesis of the Nazi approach, which valued brawn over brain, and were disliked by Hitler.

Mentally and physically, therefore, Baldur von Schirach seemed an unusual character to find in Nazi company. However, behind his cultured exterior and polite manners, he concealed a strong will, great organising ability and the knack of enthusing young men and boys with ideals of comradeship, patriotism and honour. Where an older leader might have met youthful resistance, von Schirach was more like an admired elder brother whose siblings longed to emulate him.

Von Schirach was only 22 when he became head of the National Socialist German Students' League in 1929. His brief from Hitler was to impose Nazi control over the whole university system. As if this task were not monumental enough, a special post was created for him under a directive from Hitler

Left: Young German boys are lured by the experience of firing a machine-gun. Weapons-related activities were useful recruitment devices for the Hitler Youth organisation.

dated 30 October 1931: von Schirach was now *Reichsjugendführer*, (Reich Youth Leader of the Nazi Party) so that, at 24, combined with his leadership of the Hitler Youth, he possessed infinitely more power and scope than Gruber had ever enjoyed. Von Schirach showed his Nazi steel straight away, and used the brutal, bullying methods he had learned in the SA to oust any youth leaders he considered insufficiently devoted to the Führer.

His next task was to mobilise the youth to campaign for Hitler and the Nazi party in a spate of elections which took place in 1932. By this time, six years of rigorous training was well on the way to turning the Hitler Youth into a body of boys adept at obeying orders, steeped in hatred of Jews and other 'pariahs', and willing to use violence to deal with the enemies of the Führer. Not surprisingly, the movement was organised like an army with heraldic emblems, such as flags, uniforms and insignia, and 'regiments' with a capacity for as many as 375,000 boys. There was a hierarchy of ranks. A boy who started out as a humble *Pimpf* (boy) in the *Jungvolk* could rise to lead a squad, platoon, company, battalion and finally, become a *Jungbannführer* (leader of the regiment). Ranks in the Hitler Youth itself

Right: Hitler Youth Leader Baldur von Schirach exchanges salutes with the Führer on the dais after the Hitler Youth line up for inspection at the Nazi Party Rally held at Nuremberg on 12 September 1936. Von Schirach hero-worshipped Hitler and wrote admiring poems in his honour. He would remain as Hitler Youth leader until 1943, and unlike his beloved Führer, survived the war.

Above: A 'propaganda wagon' full of Hitler Youth drives through Berlin on 19 August 1934. The banner reads: 'The Führer commands, we follow. Everyone says Yes!'

were the same, but there were further rungs beyond regimental leader to divisional, district and main district leader and the top rank of *Stabsführer* (Leader).

Life in the Youth

Aspirations towards higher ranks and more power within the Hitler Youth were positively encouraged. The whole structure was built on aggressive competition between individuals or groups, while at the same time creating the cohesion of comradeship which characterised military life. Winning or succeeding were the only things that mattered. Parade-ground drilling, arduous but effective, was used to drum discipline into young minds. The full panoply of war – military music, drums, flags, banners and marches in which thousands of youths paraded as one – were employed to create a mass mentality infused through and through with patriotic fervour.

When unleashed on the streets in the election campaigns of 1932, the effectiveness of Hitler Youth training immediately became apparent. Politically, this was an extremely busy year, with the presidential election fixed for 13 March and for the Reichstag on 31 July. Despite his advanced age of 84, the incumbent president and war-hero, von Hindenburg, announced on 15 February that he would seek re-election. Hitler declared himself a candidate a week later.

The campaigns that followed were, inevitably, marked by extreme violence. It could hardly have been otherwise when the chief rivals fighting the Reichstag elections were two such opposite and inimical groups as the communists and the Nazis. Street brawling already typified the activities of the SA, and the Communists had their own answer to the Brownshirts – the Red Front – as well as their equivalent of the Hitler Youth. Even before the elections of 1932, the Hitler Youth, in effect the junior SA, had staged ferocious battles against young communists, using fists, knives or sticks. Before long, these confrontations degenerated into shooting matches.

There were, of course, fatalities. Twenty-three Hitler Youths were killed in street fighting between 1931 and 1933, and in 1932 the movement acquired an icon to match Horst Wessel, the young SA leader who died in a street brawl in Berlin in 1930. He was Herbert Norkus, aged 12, the son of a taxi driver from the Berlin district of Beuselkietz. Norkus was a member of a party of Hitler Youth led by Baldur von Schirach which, on Sunday morning, 26 January 1932, was posting notices of an anti-communist Nazi Party meeting to be held four days later. Suddenly, a menacing group of young communists appeared and attacked them.

Von Schirach and most of the Hitler Youth managed to escape along the surrounding

Above: Jürghen Ohlsen starred as the hero of the popular film Hitlerjunge Quex, *based on Herbert Norkus, the 12-year-old Hitler Youth killed by communists in Berlin in 1932.*

streets, but Norkus was cornered. Knives came out and Norkus was stabbed twice. His wounds streaming blood, he managed to reach a nearby house and hammered on the door for help. The door was opened, but once the occupier realised what was happening, he quickly shut it, leaving Norkus helpless and alone. Backed up against the wall, he was knifed another five times and collapsed to the ground. As he tried to get up, he left a line of bloodstained handprints on the nearby brickwork. Still alive, he was dragged along the street and dumped in the nearby Zwinglistrasse, where he died. A subsequent postmortem revealed extensive injuries. Norkus had suffered two stab wounds in the chest and three in the back, his upper lip had been cut off and his face was mutilated.

Hitlerjunge Quex

In 1933, a film entitled *Hitlerjunge Quex* ('quex' meaning 'quicksilver') was made by Ufa, Germany's most prominent studio, telling the story of Norkus' short life and violent end. It was the first to be made under the aegis of Baldur von Schirach and the Nazi government, who later used the cinema as a regular means of educating the young in the principles of National Socialism. *Hitlerjunge Quex* featured several of the Berlin Hitler Youth turned amateur actors for the occasion.

Like the eponymous novel by Karl Aloys Schenzinger on which it was based, the film idealised the dead boy and wove around him the mantle of a martyr to the Nazi cause. The closing shots of the film cunningly promoted the Nazi propaganda message: in place of the squalid real-life scene of the bloodstained Norkus dying in a Berlin street, the boy's corpse dissolved into a fluttering flag which served as the 'screen' on which scenes of Nazi activities were projected.

The novel, which Schenzinger wrote in only four months, was serialised in the *Völkischer Beobachter* before publication in December 1932. It afterwards became required reading for all German youth. Nazi propaganda went much further than this. The death of Norkus

Above: Members of the **Jungvolk,** *the junior Hitler Youth, listen attentively at a meeting in 1933. They carry the banners which played such an important part in Nazi symbolism.*

was the subject of emotional public speeches and memorial services accompanied by marches and demonstrations and he was given his own 'saint's day', 24 January, which was kept as a special day of mourning to commemorate all Hitler Youth who had died in Nazi service.

The Weimar authorities took a much more jaundiced view of both the Norkus incident and the whole business of street violence during the elections. Official alarm increased after first results in the presidential election, on 13 March 1932, seemed to hold potential for even more trouble; the venerable Paul von Hindenburg had not received the required majority and a second ballot would have to take place. The date chosen was 10 April. That same month, the Weimar government outlawed both the SA and the Hitler Youth. The ban on the Hitler Youth backfired: a wave of new recruits flocked to the movement. The ban held good for only a short while, and had no effect on Hitler Youth campaigning, which was tireless. All over Germany, the Youth distributed leaflets and pamphlets by the million, together with special editions of the *Völkischer Beobachter,* or otherwise publicised the Nazi cause in marches and parades.

Von Hindenburg managed to secure the presidency again on 10 April, though with far less of a majority – 53 per cent – than a hero of his lustre could have expected. Hitler, with nearly 37 per cent of the vote – almost three times as much as the Communist candidate – pronounced the result a victory for National Socialism. A much more real victory lay ahead on 31 July, when the Nazis doubled their seats in the Reichstag to 230, becoming the largest single party.

Massive rally

Two months later, on 2 October, Baldur von Schirach greeted this success with the greatest display by the Hitler Youth and other youth organisations that Germany had ever seen. Von Schirach summoned the entire membership under his command to travel to Potsdam for a *Reichsjugendtage der NSDAP* (a Reich Youth Day rally of the Nazi Party). Some 100,000 youths responded and travelled to Potsdam, many of them on foot. Hitler was visibly affected as they marched past in a continuous stream that took seven hours, from eleven in the morning to six in the evening, to pass by his review stand.

Although their victory at the polls on 31 July had not given the Nazis a majority over all other parties, Adolf Hitler was now very close to realising the power he had craved for so long. In the ensuing months, several attempts were made to form a government that would exclude the Nazis, but given the latter's huge presence in the Reichstag, they all failed. Eventually, at the end of 1932, Fritz von Papen suggested that Hitler become Chancellor of Germany, with himself as Vice-Chancellor. Von Papen fancied he could control Hitler and so claim the real power in Germany. Just how wrong he was became clear in a very short time. Though extremely reluctant to do so, President Hindenburg summoned Hitler to the presidential palace in Berlin. There, at midday on 30 January 1933, the gallant old soldier offered the man he so detested and feared the second highest office in the state. Hitler accepted.

Celebrations

Berlin exploded in noisy celebration that night, with the Hitler Youth out in force in the streets of Berlin, taking part alongside the SA and other Nazi organisations in triumphal torchlight processions and parades through the capital. Although Hitler did not yet have total power in Germany – for that, he had to wait until President von Hindenberg died in 1934 – von Schirach's ambitions for the Hitler Youth could now go forward. His goal was nothing less than to bring the whole of German youth under his own aegis and turn them all into dedicated Nazis.

His first move was to get rid of the competition. In 1933, there were about 400 youth groups still outside the Nazi fold and von Schirach began at the core of this opposition, the Reich Committee of German Youth Associations. The Associations represented about six million German youngsters, providing them with a full range of youth activities, education and facilities. Independent control of this appreciable organisation was wiped out in a few minutes on 3 April 1933, when von Schirach ordered 50 members of the Hitler Youth to enter its Berlin headquarters and take over its offices, its staff and its assets. That done, employees were told that their organisation was under new, Nazi, management. Not for long. In less than three months, their jobs would disappear as von Schirach and the Nazi Party used terror and the threat of terror to absorb or destroy all other youth groups in Germany.

Von Schirach promoted

Von Schirach was soon riding higher than ever before. On 17 June 1933, Hitler appointed him *Jugendführer des Deutschen Reiches* (Youth Leader of Germany), answerable directly to Hitler himself. This promotion placed all youth groups and their activities under von Schirach's control. One of his first acts was to dissolve the 'defunct' Reichs Committee of German Youth Associations. Other groups were handled no less brutally. Jewish and communist groups were soon disbanded and the headquarters of the Socialist Workers' Youth was raided. The Socialist Youth, originally founded before 1906, was a particular target because it was already highly politicised, with well established links to Denmark, the Netherlands and Sweden among other European countries. The movement had commended itself to ordinary Germans during the economic hardships of 1930 and

Right: Members of the Hitler Youth stand to attention. They wear badges typical of their organisation – the Sig Rune 'S', symbol of victory – and daggers at their waists.

afterwards by forming a special emergency service to help the unemployed. This Socialist Youth was therefore a strong rival to the Nazis and the Hitler Youth and as such, had to be expunged. Its leaders could see quite clearly that what was happening to other movements would soon happen to them, and so large sections disbanded voluntarily before the Nazis did it for them. Subsequently, members of the former Socialist Youth joined the resistance to the Third Reich.

Many Christian organisations went the other way. They came under strong pressure to join the Nazi youth movement, and most of the Protestant groups yielded quickly enough. This was a major coup for the Nazis: the Protestant, mainly Lutheran and Reformed, church comprised some 68 per cent of the German

Above: A group of smiling young girls salute Hitler, while others wait to present their bouquets. Girls were expected to grow up to be good housewives with large families.

population and 99 per cent of all Protestants in Germany. Meanwhile, Hitler's friend, Chaplain Ludwig Mueller, was manoeuvred into place as the first Reich Bishop for the obvious purpose of Nazifying the Protestant Church.

The Catholic Church in Germany proved a rather tougher opponent. German Catholics were backed by the formidable power of an international organisation and the influence of a major world figure, Eugene Pacelli, Pope Pius XII. In addition, devout Catholics could already be found in the higher ranks of the Nazi Party and in the Hitler Youth. They regularly attended Mass, and some of the Youth were choirboys, wearing their church robes over their Hitler Youth uniforms. The Nazi government recognised – or appeared to

recognise – the importance of Catholicism in Germany when on 20 July 1933, a concordat with the Vatican was ratified. Under this arrangement, the government guaranteed freedom of Catholic worship in Germany and the right of the Church to regulate its own affairs.

The Catholics suppressed
It took only 10 days for the Nazis to renege. On 30 July, the first moves were made towards dismantling the Catholic Youth League. This, though, was only the start of a persecution of Catholics in which priests, nuns and other officials were hounded, or falsely charged with crimes. Church newspapers and other publications were suppressed and the Gestapo, the Nazi secret police, invaded the confessional in the so-called interests of the state. On 19 November 1935, the Gestapo occupied the central office of the Catholic Youth in Düsseldorf and, after searching it,

closed it down. Shortly afterwards, the Catholic Youth magazine, *Michael*, which had a circulation of 300,000, was likewise closed down. Though the Catholic Youth Movement managed to survive for three years, those years were marked by regular street battles with the Hitler Youth, especially in Catholic areas like the Rhineland.

Meanwhile, other youth groups disintegrated under intense Nazi pressure. Within six months of Hitler's assumption of power, 20 youth leagues representing a majority of Germany's youth organisations, both religious and political, had either been dismantled or were being terrorised into submission. Not surprisingly the combined membership of the Hitler Youth, the *Jungvolk* and the *Bund*

Deutscher Mädel (the League of German Girls), rocketed once the Nazis came to power and other youth movements were voluntarily, or forcibly, absorbed. The total of 107,956 in 1932 soared to 2,292,041 in 1933 and went on rising until the brink of World War II in 1939, when it stood at 7,287,470.

The Hitler Youth restructured
Having levelled the playing field, von Schirach set about restructuring the Hitler Youth. He shifted the age groups slightly, so that boys were in the *Jungvolk*, the 'junior' Hitler Youth, between the ages of 10 and 14. At 14, the children moved up into the Hitler Youth and remained there until the age of 18. Although the purpose of the girls' league was intended to

Right: Having displaced traditional Christian influence in the Third Reich, the Nazi party attempted to provide a neo-pagan substitute, the **Deutsche Glaubensbewegung** *(the German Faith Movement). Here, Ludwig Müller, the proponent of the Faith Movement and Hitler's personal choice as Reich bishop, salutes a Nazi gathering.*

prepare females for the traditional life of domesticity, motherhood and nothing else, its members were not given soft options. The girls wore special uniforms of skirts and blouses, but were also required to possess hiking boots. The physical training of girls was vital, it was thought, for their future chances of healthy pregnancies producing healthy children, and they were just as subject as the boys to fitness regimes, long hikes through the countryside,

and sports competitions. The toughening-up process for both sexes even went so far as to keep them short of food from time to time, in order to harden their resolve and build up resilience. For both sexes a strong element of competition in every activity – sports, collecting money, neatly written reports or records, spotless hygiene – was used as the spur which drove them to excel.

Under von Schirach's new rules, boys were informally introduced into the youth movement at the age of six. The tendency of very young boys to hang around their near-elders, admiring and envying their skills and longing to be like them, was cleverly used as a preliminary to formal entry into the *Jungvolk*. The *Jungvolk* were not pampered or treat lightly in any way. On entering the organisation, they were required to swear a terrifying oath which impressed on them the responsibility they bore. The oath was sworn on the *Blutfahne* (Blood Banner), a Nazi 'icon' said to have been soaked in the blood of those who had died in the failed putsch of 1923. At the Nuremberg rallies, all new flags were touched to this grim relic. 'In the presence of this blood banner, which represents our Führer,' the oath ran, 'I swear to devote all my energies and my strength to the saviour of our country, Adolf Hitler. I am willing and ready to give up my life for him, so help me God!'

The Year of the Jungvolk

Von Schirach, who was constantly devising ways to please his hero, Hitler, termed 1936 as *Der Jahre das Jungvolk* (the Year of the *Jungvolk*). More specifically, it was the year when he planned to give Hitler a birthday present which comprised nothing less than all the 10-year olds in Germany. In order to achieve this considerable ambition, Nazi teachers in school pressured their pupils to join the *Jungvolk*, parents were summoned to

Left: Music formed a significant part of the Hitler Youth's display at rallies. Most of the tunes they played came from traditional German working songs and ballads.

Above: The Land Service was aimed at removing urban youth from the 'unhealthy' towns and 'returning' them to the delights of working on the land.

special meetings designed to make them influence their children, and the Hitler Youth staged marches and parades to get the message across.

On the 'great day' itself, 20 April 1936, Hitler's 47th birthday, the oath-taking ceremony took place inside the imposing Marienburg Castle. The Castle had once been the headquarters of the Teutonic Order, a religious organisation of knights who had participated in the crusades in the twelfth century. The soaring ancient walls loomed out of a half-darkness, lit only by flickering torchlights. Drums sounded and trumpets fanfared as each 10-year-old stepped forward to take his oath. The ceremony ended with the singing of *Fahnenlied* (the Banner Song), which von Schirach had written as the Hitler Youth anthem:

> Our banner flutters before us
> Our banner represents a new era
> And our banner leads to eternity!
> Yes, our banner means more to us
> than death!

Early training in the *Jungvolk* was conducted by some of the older members of the Hitler Youth. It was their task to prepare

Above: These young men, parading with their spades held like a rifle, demonstrate their belief that their every action contributed to the glory of the Third Reich; even digging.

the 10-year-olds for tests which would ensure that only the most excellent among them would enter the Hitler Youth itself. The youngsters had to recite the verses of the 'Horst Wessel Song', written by the SA 'Brownshirt' of that name who had been killed in 1930. Reputedly based on a Salvation Army hymn, the 'Horst Wessel', which stood second only to the national anthem, became the Nazis' marching song.

Next, the *Jungvolk* were required to give the correct answers to questions on Nazi racial, political and other ideology and on the history of the Party. The boys' physical fitness was tested by requirements to run 60 metres in 12 seconds, throw a baseball, accomplish a demanding long jump and complete a cross-country hike which could last as long as three days. Finally, they had to demonstrate their courage by jumping from the first or second storey of a building into a large sheet of canvas held taut by members of the Hitler Youth. Once this *Mutprobe* (courage test) was satisfactorily completed, a 10-year-old was entitled to wear the uniform: brown shirt decorated with the insignia of the *Jungvolk*, a leather shoulder strap, and the Hitler Youth dagger, which was inscribed with the phrase 'Blut und Ehre' ('Blood and Honour'). 'In this first test,' the new recruits were told, 'you fulfil your duty for the first time. You do so with pleasure, because millions of your young comrades do the same. You have become a soldier of Adolf Hitler!'

New recruits into the *Jungvolk* were so young that they had barely begun to think for themselves. This made it relatively easy for von Schirach to mould them in the required Nazi image. However, there was a problem with the older boys who had joined the Hitler Youth from movements absorbed by the Nazis, and did not have the advantage of a *Jungvolk* apprenticeship behind them. Rapidly increased membership of the Hitler Youth from 55,365 in 1932 to 568,288 by the close of 1933 meant that many of them were, as yet, untrained in the Nazi mind-set and unused to the strict discipline and demanding regimen of the Hitler Youth. There were, in addition, too few properly trained, suitably Nazified young men able to lead them effectively.

Leadership schools

Von Schirach tackled this problem by setting up *Reichsführer* schools which offered crash courses in leadership, Nazi racial beliefs and Nazified German history. Training in rifle shooting and vigorous physical activity were included in the brief, three-week, programme. By the summer of 1934, after less than a year, von Schirach was able to report to Hitler that this quick-fix regime had produced 12,000 new leaders for the Hitler Youth and double that number for the *Jungvolk*.

In 1934, which he termed 'The Year of Training', von Schirach expressed the principles by which unpromising material could be turned into reliable leaders in such a short time. 'Whoever marches in the Hitler Youth is not a number among millions, but the soldier of an idea,' he said. 'The individual member's value to the whole is determined by the degree to which he is permeated by the idea. The best Hitler Youth, irrespective of rank or office, is he who completely surrenders himself to the National Socialist world view'.

Training

A Hitler Youth was not intended merely as the 'soldier of an idea'. He was always destined to fight real, hot war on behalf of the Third Reich. The emphasis on arduous physical activity, comradeship and blind devotion to the Führer was intended to harden young men for this

Above: Members of the marine Hitler Youth flank a Nazi swastika at the 8th Nazi Party Rally, 8–14 September 1936. From the podium, von Schirach addresses the crowd.

purpose. However, as long as peace lasted, the battle to restore the name and reputation of Germany had to be fought in other ways. The Hitler Youth was set to learning trades, working on farms or in private homes, planting trees and flowers to beautify the parks, or rebuilding roads, singing in youth choirs and taking part in music festivals. Some of the boys concentrated on bettering the lives of rural children, who were relatively deprived in the 1930s compared to their town counterparts. For them, the Hitler Youth provided medical and dental care, hygiene facilities such as showers, and exercise programmes to build up their health and physique.

The Hitler Youth were required to show a great deal more empathy with the countryside

Below: The Nuremberg Rally of 1936 showing von Schirach in the foreground, saluting as he inspects the ranks of his Hitler Youth. The 1936 rally attracted worldwide attention.

than the occasional rural excursion for hiking or sports or giving help to the disadvantaged. One of the most potent Nazi slogans, 'Blut und Boden' ('Blood and Soil'), was a banner under which the Hitler Youth were supposed to lead a move away from the towns, with their artificial temptations, back to the rural life where the 'noble peasant' worked the soil in tune with nature. There, untainted by the metropolitan mixture of the towns where Jews congregated, the peasants preserved the racially pure ethos of Aryan superiority.

This 'back-to-the-land' ideal predated Hitler's rise to power, originating from the right-wing Artamanen movement created in 1924 by Albert Wojirsch, an industrial machinist who joined the Nazi party three years later. Members of the Artamanen included Richard Walther Darré, an agrarian expert, and his friend Heinrich Himmler, who became chief of the SS in 1929. In April 1933, Darré, who headed the agrarian department

within the SS, was appointed by Hitler as *Reichsbauernführer* (Reich Agricultural Leader) and *Reichsernährungminister* (Reich Food Minister). Eighteen months later, Artur Axmann, who headed the Social Office of the National Youth Directorate, persuaded von Schirach to admit the Artamanen movement into the Hitler Youth as the *Landdienst* (Land Service). Initially the Land Service of the Hitler Youth was fairly small – only 500 in 1934 – but this soon increased and more than 6600 Youth were involved by 1936.

Though it went against the prevailing demographic trend, the Land Service appeared very attractive. It involved working on farms from springtime till harvest time. During the winter, the Hitler Youth dispersed, some to leadership schools or agrarian institutes, some remaining on the farms. Others got together in travelling groups, going from village to village providing theatrical entertainment and spreading the message of 'Blut und Boden' among the rural communities who were otherwise largely cut off from mainstream Nazi ideology. They returned to the towns to recount their farming experiences at meetings and to propagate the ideal of 'noble' agricultural labour. Ultimately, the Hitler Youth of the Land Service were destined to settle in the countryside and found farms and families. Another purpose was to relocate jobless city youth. By the start of 1935, some 200,000 young people had been removed from idleness in the towns to do temporary work on farms. There, according to Albert Wojitsch, 'severe discipline, simple lifestyle, hard work and daily duties' would give them a sense of purpose in keeping with Nazi principles and nullify the corrosive effect of urban idleness.

Propaganda

The smiling, healthy, bronzed youth labouring happily in the fields provided Nazi propaganda with some of its most impressive photo-opportunities. The whole picture was of a vast body of youth united in discipline and the pursuit of excellence, proud of their national heritage, diligent in all tasks assigned them and above all, obedient to authority. As the Nazi Party had fully intended when it propagated this rosy scenario, the outside world was impressed. What was not apparent, however, was the motive power of racism and repression that lay behind these scenes. In an age when there was no world-wide media or instant communications of the power and scope of later in the century, the Nazi propaganda machine had a relatively clear field to peddle its message. It was so potent that it created a political blindness abroad about the reality of Nazi Germany. Many foreigners who realised later, and too late, that they should have known better – like David Lloyd George, British Prime Minister during World War I – returned from visits to Germany full of praise and enthusiasm for the metamorphosis the Nazis had wrought there.

Hidden terror

The metamorphosis was real enough, but what visitors saw was what the Nazi Party wanted them to see: a burgeoning economy in place of poverty and despair, full employment, mighty new industries risen from the ashes of war, improving health standards and splendid leisure facilities. Beneath the carefully contrived patina of success and the Nazi 'miracle', the less salubrious aspects of a state ruled by terror, persecution and repression were carefully concealed from foreign view.

In the Hitler Youth, one aspect hidden from foreign eyes was the *Hitlerjugend-Streifendienst* (Patrol Service) which acted like a junior Gestapo. They kept order at Hitler Youth meetings, often by beating up troublemakers in the now-traditional Brownshirt manner. They spied out suspect loyalties and reported anyone who spoke against Hitler or the Nazi Party, even as a joke. Patrol Force members were capable of denouncing their own parents on occasion. The father of Walter Hess, a Hitler Youth member in Wittlich near the French border, ended up in Dachau concentration camp – where he died – after his son revealed that he had described Hitler as a 'crazed maniac'.

Above: Elaborate and impressive ceremony played an important part in the induction of the Jungvolk, as it did in every Nazi Party public display. Here, 10-year-olds line up for roll-call before ceremonies begin.

Young Hess, meanwhile, received a promotion for his service to the Reich.

Leaders of surviving non-Nazi youth groups forced to operate underground found themselves arrested on the initiative of Patrol

Service infiltrators. The Service's operatives were also involved in the purge of 30 June 1934, the so-called 'Night of the Long Knives', when Ernst Röhm and over 1000 Brownshirts of the SA were murdered on Hitler's orders. That night, Hitler settled old scores with 'traitors' like the 72-year-old Gustav von Kahr, who had put down the Nazi putsch of 1923, and the leader of the Catholic Youth, Adalbert Probst, as well as other youth leaders who were rivals to the Hitler Youth.

The formula for these developments and the metamorphosis of youth into an efficient, obedient and, where necessary, ruthless fighting machine was set out in 'The Law Concerning the Hitler Youth', dated 1 December 1936, which stated:

The future of the German nation depends on its youth. The whole of German youth must therefore be prepared for its future duties. The Reich Government has accordingly decided on the following law ... The whole of German youth within the frontiers of the Reich is organised in the Hitler Youth. The whole of German youth is to be educated, outside the parental home and school, in the Hitler Youth physically, intellectually and morally in the spirit of National Socialism for service to the nation and the community.

The same Law rescinded the concordat of 1933 with the Vatican. This put an end to the Catholic Youth Organisation which had managed to hang on in Germany, despite intense Nazi harassment, for three years.

Its demise at last gave the Nazi Party a monopoly of youth organisations, as had long been intended, and was one reason why there was an immense rise in membership to 5,437,601 by 1936. Another was the pursuit of parents who were threatened with fines, heavy prison sentences or with losing their children if they tried to keep them from the compulsory Hitler Youth meetings: this was classed as being 'politically unreliable'. Parents also qualified for punishment if they had Jewish friends or belonged to the Jehovah's Witnesses,

another persecuted group. Hitler Youth leaders even distributed special questionnaires asking secondary school students to list infractions not only by parents, but also by teachers and employers.

Sometimes the boys themselves produced the desired result by emotional blackmail. It was not unknown for *Pimpfen* in the *Jungvolk* whose parents were insufficiently Nazified to be refused promotion into the Hitler Youth. This meant that the boys had no future in the Nazi state. This prospect was so fearful that there were boys who preferred to attempt suicide. Rather than have their boys throw away their lives, frightened parents would take steps to hide their anti-Nazi sentiments or even join in Nazi activities both to prove their loyalty and secure promotion for their sons.

Feared influence

Parental resistance persisted nevertheless. It was understandable. The Hitler Youth was the one influence parents most feared, an influence that would alienate their children and fill their heads with ideas they detested. Rather than that, a few parents chose to emigrate and take their families to a healthier social and political climate abroad. It was also insurance for themselves: the fate of Walter Hess's father was a grim warning to all of them.

Below: Rousing patriotic songs and anthems were regularly sung at the rallies, round the campfires or at meetings by the **Jungvolk** *and the* **Hitler Youth.**

LIFE IN THE HITLER YOUTH

Life in the Hitler Youth was a carefully planned combination of energetic activity, excitement, discipline, compulsion and indoctrination, with particular emphasis placed on the ideal of physical perfection dedicated to the greater glory of the Fatherland. Whatever the activity, the entire Hitler Youth system was infused with military values. This went beyond the obvious of the uniforms, the ranks, the drilling or the parades. Even the lessons in the superiority of the Aryan Master Race had a military slant, by providing 'enemies' – Jews, gypsies, communists – against whom war had to be waged.

Of all Hitler Youth activities, competitive sport was by far the most important. It was not meant solely for exercise, or health or the benefits of fresh air. Sport in Nazi Germany comprised an arena in which a warlike environment was created to boost patriotism and allow boys to indulge in the sort of physical violence that was otherwise acceptable only on the battlefield. In practice, this channelled natural boyish aggression, in which pushing, shoving, fist-fighting, or

Left: The military emphasis in the Hitler Youth increased after 1939. Here boys practise on the firing ranges in 1940. Before long, boys this young would be shooting in combat.

ganging up on weaker members of a group was a normal, if painful, part of growing up.

This use of sport was not unique to Nazi Germany, of course. In England, for example, competitive sports were equally rough. There, though, they were used as lessons in fair play, team spirit or magnanimity in victory and good grace in defeat. The Nazi concept was quite different. Sport in Hitler's Germany was all about striving for excellence and forging courage and daring in order to exemplify the virtues of the Master Race.

Importance of sport

In his speeches, Adolf Hitler often emphasised the theme of a youth that must be 'slim and slender as greyhounds, tough as leather and hard as Krupp steel'. He declared:

I will have (the youth) fully trained in all physical exercises. I intend to have an athletic

Left: The natural boyish love of weapons was fully exploited when it came to sustaining enthusiasm among the Hitler Youth. Here, eager youngsters handle machine-guns.

Above: At the Nazi Party Rally in September 1937, a Hitler Youth displays his skill with a rifle. Those with a natural gift for sharp-shooting were given special encouragement.

youth, that is the first and the chief thing. In this way, I shall eradicate the thousands of years of human domestication. Then I shall have in front of me the pure and noble natural material. With that, I can create the new order ... The whole education in a national state must aim first of all not at stuffing the student with mere knowledge, but by building bodies which are healthy to the core ... I will have no intellectual training. Knowledge is ruin to my young men. A violently active, dominating, brutal youth – that is what I am after. Youth must be indifferent to pain. There must be no weakness and tenderness in it. I want to see once more in its eyes the gleam of pride and independence of the beast of prey.

In Nazi Germany, therefore, physical fitness, racial and political supremacy and the victory of the Master Race were all intertwined. The ultimate goal was to create a ruling class of

impeccable loyalty to the state, together with armed services whose prowess, military preparedness and fidelity to Germany reached a standard unknown anywhere else in the world. The Nazis were, nevertheless, realistic about the time it would take to make Hitler's ideal a reality. To them, a few months or even few years of sports and weapons training or parade-ground drilling did not make a soldier: at least 10 years' commitment was required in order to create suitable warriors for whom handling weapons was a natural function and devotion to the Nazi cause was as automatic as breathing.

Special schools

In addition, the future leaders of the Nazi state were to be trained in three special schools set up after 1933. The *Adolf Hitler Schule* (Adolf Hitler Schools) were intended to train the Nazi elite, and the *Nationalpolitische Erziehungsanstalten* (National Political Training Institutes, or 'Napolas') were to be run along the lines of the old Prussian academies to provide manpower for high government posts. Here, candidates were to be inculcated with 'soldierly spirit, with attributes of courage, sense of duty and simplicity'. First set up as early as April 1933, there were 23 'Napolas' by 1938, four of them in Austria and one in the Sudetenland. The third type of establishment was the *Ordensburgen* (Order Castles) which were finishing schools for future Nazi Party leaders. At the *Ordensburgen*, Robert Ley, the organisational chief of the Nazi Party, instructed that 'there must be great attention paid to riding because it gives the Junkers [the old Prussian aristocracy] the feeling of being able to dominate a living creature entirely'.

Whether for the élite few or the ordinary masses of Hitler Youth, von Schirach, brimming with ideas and how to organise them, knew exactly how to make Hitler's

Left: Bronzed Hitler Youth play on a beach by the Baltic. Sports, played almost to the point of exhaustion, built up not only healthy bodies, but also discipline and team spirit.

dream of an 'athletic youth' come true. Hitler Youth training involved long hikes through the countryside and the active pursuit of almost every conceivable sport: running, jumping, boxing, throwing the discus and the hammer, swimming, gymnastics, and all manner of ball games.

More overtly military sports included target shooting, and small calibre rifles were provided for the Hitler Youth. Initially introduced for the enjoyment of handling weapons and developing a good eye and a steady hand for accuracy, target sports were an obvious stepping-stone towards similar expertise in war. Even the *Jungvolk* were trained in skills useful to soldiers, such as signalling by semaphore, repairing bicycles, laying telephone cables, and using dummy hand grenades, air guns and smaller bore rifles. These activities could be classed, conveniently, as sports, and so did not contravene the ban imposed at Versailles on overtly military preparations. Target shooting was, after all, a recognised Olympic sport.

However, even after the ban ceased to have meaning, in 1935, when German re-armament and war training were no longer secrets, the Nazis sought ways to obscure anything that could be seen as warlike. Already, sailing, flying and gliding clubs had been used in this context, as was orienteering, in which the Hitler Youth were trained to read maps, recognise landmarks, judge distances, camouflage themselves, and reconnoitre the terrain.

No quarter given

In this, as in all youth activities, intensity of competition was always paramount. Several ways were provided to give a constant buzz of excitement and challenge. One was the pace at which sports were played, often to the point of exhaustion, in order to build up toughness and determination. No quarter was given to the weaker boys who were always present in any group. They were, for example, deliberately made to suffer in a hide-and-seek game called 'Trapper and Indian'. Played by two teams, one with red and one with blue arm bands, the idea was to trail and trap the 'enemy' team, and defeat them by ripping off their arm bands.

Below: The girls of the **Bund Deutscher Mädel,** *like this young fencer, were not spared hard physical exercise. In the Nazi Party ethos, active sports benefited their future.*

This offered plenty of opportunity for playing rough, something the *Scharführeren* (platoon leaders) actively encouraged. They would stand by as some of the boys were punched, pummelled, thrown to the ground, had their shirts ripped and got thoroughly bloody noses, all in the cause of teaching them to be more aggressive next time.

Above: Air enthusiasts among the Hitler Youth joined the **Flieger-Hitlerjugend.** *At first, training consisted of building and flying model gliders, learning the principles of flight.*

Under von Schirach's direction, sports in the Third Reich were systematically organised and were given maximum publicity throughout Germany. Instruction books were issued detailing the activities appropriate to all age groups and both sexes. Among other, more general purposes within the Hitler Youth, these served as guide books for supervisors at the leadership schools which were set up in all areas of the country.

Weekend camps

The weekend camps where the Hitler Youth received much of their sports and other training had a particular purpose. Here, the boys could be under control and away from distracting outside influences, such as their parents. Here, too, class differences could be ironed out, as the boys shared the same conditions, endured the same bad weather, lived in tents or huts, slept in dormitories, ate the same food, made the same efforts and built up a camaraderie that, ideally, had nothing to

do with differing family circumstances. There was, in addition, equal opportunity to win 'achievement medals', another of von Schirach's innovations to promote competition. Open to members of the Hitler Youth, *Jungvolk, Bund Deutscher Mädel* and the *Jungmädelgruppen* (the groups for younger girls), the medals became coveted trophies and the high profile which sport was given in Nazi propaganda ensured that winners of these awards became junior national heroes and heroines.

Annual showpiece event

The National Sports Competition, introduced in 1935 – named by von Schirach as 'The Year of Physical Training' – was the big annual showpiece of Hitler Youth activities. Spurred on to compete by the many incentives on offer, more and more young people took part, rising from 1.5 million in 1933 to seven million by 1939. During the first year of the competition,

Above: It was not all hard work for the **Flieger-Hitlerjugend.** *Here they watch a four-engined transport, the Junkers-38, take off from a runway before the war.*

there was the additional excitement of the 1936 Olympic Games held in Berlin. Results at the Games enabled Nazi propaganda to glorify the ideal of the physically perfect youth when Germans won gold medals in 16 different sports including four for gymnastics and six for rowing.

At this juncture, the Nazis were still striving to conceal their anti-Jewish policies from the outside world, and some token Jewish athletes were allowed to take part in the Games. This window-dressing, however, fronted a systematic programme of classroom education designed to make German children aware of the 'Jewish canker' in their midst. Lessons in school filled the heads of the Hitler Youth with ideas of Aryan superiority which were just as potent as those inculcated on the sportsfield. All classes took place under the glowering presence of Hitler's portrait and the 'history' taught there glorified the Munich putsch of 1923, and the Führer's struggle to free Germany from the insidious influence of Jews, capitalists and communists.

This unabashed propaganda had been promulgated by Hitler himself together with a veiled reference to Nazi plans to exterminate the Jews. 'It is the task of the racial state', Hitler declared, 'to ensure that at long last world history will be written and that, within its context, the racial question will be elevated to the dominant position ... so that a generation will emerge capable of facing the final and decisive decision on this globe.'

Jewish isolation

The first important lesson to be learned was how to spot a Jew. For a time, Jewish children were still allowed to attend school, and they were used as specimens, standing before the class, while the teacher pointed out certain racial characteristics: shape of nose, shape and size of head, set of eyes, skin colour and so on. Particular attention was paid to the low forehead, long skull, short, weakling physique and the fact that Jewish boys were circumcised. For contrast and to emphasise the lesson, pure Nordic and Germanic types also stood up in front of the class to be analysed. Their characteristics, classes were told, made them a 'chosen race' created in the image of God to possess power, knowledge, culture and the talent for organisation. This instruction was backed up by textbooks, one of which had a chapter entitled 'Characteristic and Distinguishing Features of Jews', and photographs of Jews, in profile and full-face like prisoners in custody, hung on the walls. Demonstrations were given of Jewish body language, and the way they gesticulated with their hands.

In these ways, young Germans were progressively steeped in the 'perils' of Jewish contamination, as expressed in Hitler Youth songs which contained lines like: 'When Jewish blood splashes from the knives, things will go doubly well'. Eventually, the national education system, both elementary and secondary, was replaced by the Hitler Youth and its teachers and instructors. Jews were dismissed from their university and other teaching posts, and in 1936, the Roman Catholic and Protestant schools were closed. This left the field free for the dissemination of Nazi ideas, which included not only hatred of the Jews, but also other groups such as gypsies, Slavs and other 'undesirables'.

Policy for the disabled

Among them were the disabled. Here, a line was drawn between the mentally and the physically disabled. The latter were, in fact, allowed to join the Disabled and Infirm Hitler Youth as long as they passed the racial tests. They took no part, of course, in the sports or the paramilitary training, but they learned useful skills such as carpentry, light manual work or clerical work. Even the blind and the deaf were admitted to Hitler Youth ranks – as long as their disabilities were not inherited.

The mentally disabled were quite another matter. To produce a Master Race, the Nazis believed, it was necessary to weed out the feeble-minded, the insane, epileptics, schizo-phrenics, the malformed, the congenitally blind and deaf and and chronic alcoholics. All of them were liable to be sterilised or quietly put to death under the euthanasia programme run by the Nazis.

To impress the Hitler Youth with the need to cleanse society of these undesirables, groups were taken to hospitals and institutions where they saw for themselves how much mental illness was costing the country, and how much more it would cost if such people were allowed to produce equally 'faulty' children. 'You should produce children only with pure Germans to avoid bringing criminals or disabled people into the world' the Hitler Youth were told in an edition of *You and Your People*, the movement's newsletter. 'The sterilisation law allows us ... to exercise human dignity and not subject our race to inferiority.'

The newsletter and other printed matter circulated among the Hitler Youth was produced by the movement's own experts in journalism, broadcasting and film-making. Even though the emphasis in the Hitler Youth was away from individualism and towards group consciousness, their talents were of evident use in Nazi Germany and promising youngsters were given the chance to develop their skills. Hitler had already proved how potent public speaking could be and a great deal of his success in rising to power was attributed, rightly, to his genius for powerful oratory. Therefore, training public speakers became vital in order to keep up the impetus and enthuse fresh audiences with the Nazi message.

Special department

By 1936, there was a sufficiently large pool of Hitler Youth with the required understanding of the movement's culture and the ideology of Nazism for a special department to be set up devoted to training public speakers. This was attached to the propaganda department of the Reich Youth Office and was the result of an agreement with the *Reichspropagandaleitung* (RPL), the management for Reich propaganda.

Potential candidates were assessed on their ability, and the length of time they had spent in the Hitler Youth or the Nazi Party. When considered proficient, they were issued with licences from the RPL. There were three groups of Hitler Youth speakers – the Reich group, the regional and the unit speakers – together with the smallest section, the speaker circle. Neither the speaker school nor the speaker circle was expected to produce readymade practitioners of high quality, but were meant to provide a sound basis of training, a testing ground for speakers to hone their abilities and, generally, offer encouragement and backup for trainees.

Below: Going solo. This picture was used by the **Flieger-Hitlerjugend** *as part of an advertising campaign aimed at impressing the thrills of flight on potential recruits.*

Besides this, there was a great deal of homework to be done. Potential speakers had to absorb Nazi literature, read the newspapers, the magazines and the many books published on the subject of National Socialism. A Speaker Service was established to provide them with information and guidance. The wording, the impact and the success of a speech was up to the individual and much also depended on his smart appearance in uniform, his physical attractions, his qualities of voice and his ability to hold an audience.

The speaker's corps

Hitler Youth speakers who were naturally adept in this role soon made themselves known and the best of them were considered suitable to join the Nazi Party speakers' corps within a fairly short time. Some were already seasoned performers who had disseminated the Nazi message even before Hitler came to power. Training was successful enough for a predicted 100 new speakers to join the Nazi Party ranks by 1937. By then, there were a total of 550 Hitler Youth speakers whose lives consisted of moving from one campaign to the next, spreading the Nazi message at meetings and rallies and emphasising the near-mythical role of Adolf Hitler in saving Germany from its enemies.

The religious aura Hitler acquired was essential to the Nazi ethos and had great power in a country where the 'leader principle' had such unfailing appeal. In the Hitler Youth, this approach to the Führer was reflected in special prayers, one of which was modelled after 'The Lord's Prayer':

Adolf Hitler, you are our great Führer. Thy name makes the enemy tremble. Thy Third Reich comes, thy will alone is law upon the Earth. Let us hear daily thy voice and order us by thy leadership, for we will obey to the end and even with our lives. We praise thee! Heil Hitler!

This kind of devotion elevated Nazism and its Führer to the status of a new faith and its

Above: A postcard advertising the joys of being a member of the Hitler Youth. Exercises like the one shown were encouraged to develop competition and muscle strength.

prophet. The gap was simply waiting to be filled. Nazi persecution of Roman Catholics and the hold the Party exerted over the Protestant churches had removed for many citizens the basis of centuries-old religious faith in Germany. Realising that there was a spiritual need to be fulfilled, and that when they banned Christmas and Easter celebrations, there had to be suitable substitutes, the Nazis went back to pre-Christian, pagan practice with the Norse Viking Yuletide celebrations in place of Christmas. Easter was replaced by celebrations for the Spring Solstice.

The ceremonies and rituals by which religious faith was expressed lent themselves easily to new Nazi interpretations, especially when linked to military display. The Nuremberg rallies were only one example of

Above: Heinrich Himmler, head of the SS,
*inspects 12 SS-Panzerdivision **Hitlerjugend**, a*
unit which was largely formed from former
Hitler Youth members in 1943.

how readily the practice of faith and the symbolism of the Nazi Party could be brought together. In 1938, a much more modest, but nonetheless effective Ceremony of Youth was held in the Segeberg district in Holstein, northern Germany.

The proceedings began with a parade of flags which entered the meeting hall to the accompaniment of music. A poem dedicated to Adolf Hitler was read, the song 'Holy Fatherland' was sung and, after an address by the Nazi Party district leader, there was more music and the singing of the National Anthem. Finally, the national and party flags were marched slowly from the hall. The purpose of the ceremony for the children present was to mark the day they dedicated themselves to the

future of their country. Special books signed by a member of the Reichstag were presented to them in honour of the event. In all, 55 children in two groups took part in the Ceremony of the Youth, with some 1300 people in the audiences. All of them, it was reported, came of their own volition.

Ceremony of the Hitler Youth

The proceedings were much bigger and bolder at the Ceremony of the Hitler Youth. Held in 1936, this formed part of the Nuremberg Party Rally. Some 50,000 Hitler Youth marched into the stadium set aside for the ceremony which was attended by choirs, groups of instrumentalists, and members of the *Marine-Hitlerjugend* who flanked the podium prepared for the Führer. The guests of honour at the performance included Hitler's publisher, Max Amann, his private secretary, Martin Bormann, the editor and pamphleteer, Alfred Rosenberg, the head of the Nazi Labour Front,

Dr Robert Ley, as well as Hermann Göring and Admiral Erich Raeder.

Hitler arrived to an outburst of cheers, and briefly addressed the assembled Youth, before trumpets, sounding from high above on the surrounding towers, announced the start of the ceremony. A freedom song dedicated to 'Holy Germany' was sung and then the Hitler Youth field banners were slowly brought into the arena. These banners had particular significance: they had been carried through Germany on the traditional Adolf Hitler March after being dedicated at the tomb in Potsdam of the eighteenth-century King of Prussia, Frederick the Great. A single Hitler Youth, the first to enter the Nuremberg stadium, carried a blood-covered flag in memory of the 'martyred' Herbert Norkus.

As Reich Youth Leader, Von Schirach then made a speech addressed to Hitler which expressed the Hitler Youth's pride in being part of the National Socialist Movement. 'Youth has many pleasurable moments,' von Schirach declared. 'This year is the happiest of all. My Führer ... the happiness of youth is in your name. It is our immortality! Our Führer – Sieg Heil!' Hitler replied: 'These are exciting days ... We are accustomed to battle, and no attack can defeat us. You, my Youth, will always stand at my side. You will raise our flags on high! Our enemies may attempt to assault us once more, but our flag will always win the day!'

Further display

Martial music and the beating of drums sounded out before Hitler inspected the lines of Hitler Youth drawn up before him. This was followed by a fresh raising of the flags, the singing of patriotic songs, and a final drive through the stadium with Hitler standing up in his car for all to see and cheer.

The smartness, enthusiasm and dedication displayed on occasions such as this revealed an elitism which made the Hitler Youth a natural associate of the *Schutzstaffel* (SS), also

Below: Former Hitler Youth undergoing SS training, learning how to read charts and use compasses. From fairly early on, Hitler Youth training included orienteering.

known as the Black Order. Originating as Hitler's personal guard, the SS became the political police of Nazi Germany and, in the ambitions of its leader, Heinrich Himmler, had the potential to be much more. In Himmler's plans, the SS was to be built up into an army separate from, and parallel to, the Wehrmacht (the German army). By 1935, he was already eyeing the dynamic Hitler Youth as a source of recruitment. The SS was itself a youthful organisation, but the Hitler Youth was even younger. To judge by a directive of 1935, SS personnel seem to have had a lofty attitude towards their juniors. Issued by August Heissmeyer, chief of the central SS office, the directive announced: 'In order to initiate and preserve good relationships with the segments of the Hitlerjugend, the Reichsführer-SS [Himmler] wishes that all superior leaders of the Hitlerjugend should be handled in a proper and comradely fashion during ceremonial occasions.'

Although they were virtually commanded to show an interest in Hitler Youth activities,

Below: Sports were never just games to the Hitler Youth or the SS. This sports session, in 1942, was designed to toughen up recruits and prepare them for the rigours of war.

several SS leaders became enthusiastic, and came to believe that the best of the Youth would choose to join them after graduation. Until then, the SS had been only one of several destinations open to the Youth within the Nazi infrastructure. A certain amount of rivalry ensued when the *Reichsjugendführung* (RJF), the National Youth Directorate, objected to the assumption that the SS had a lien on the cream of the Hitler Youth, as did some sections of the Nazi Party when formal party membership was sidestepped by making it automatic for the Youth who joined the SS.

A closer link to the SS

The SS link with Hitler Youth was greatly boosted on 15 June 1936 when Himmler was appointed national police chief with unprecedented countrywide powers. Himmler's personal interest in the Hitler Youth escalated even further. The growing relationship was expressed in 1936 when the SS and the Hitler Youth climbed to the top of Zugspitze in the Bavarian Alps to celebrate the Summer Solstice. Von Schirach, whose sense of the symbolic was always acute, helped to organise this event. Another, similar, idea of his was an occasion on the Brocken mountain in the Harz mountains where Hitler Youth leaders

assembled to hear a speech by Himmler. The subject of this speech was apposite: it contained Himmler's plans for expanding the SS and the opportunities awaiting 18-year-olds when their Hitler Youth days came to an end.

Himmler's empire-building

In this, there was more than a whiff of personal empire-building. Himmler needed an input of between 25,000 and 30,000 new recruits a year for the SS. They had to have a doctor's certificate to prove their fitness, an important prerequisite for the arduous physical training they were to undergo. Other required checks were stringent. A criminal record meant instant rejection unless candidates had gone to prison in the cause of National Socialism before 1933. There was no place for those who wore spectacles or had less-than-perfect teeth. Likewise, the racial purity required by the SS was demanding in the extreme: candidates, Himmler told the Hitler Youth leaders, had to prove that their Aryan heritage went back untainted by 'inferior' – especially Jewish – blood over the past 11 or 12 generations, to the year 1650.

After entering the *SS-Verfügungstruppe* (SSVT), the SS Special Duty Troops, at the age of 18, the former Hitler Youth recruits would be offered experience in the other SS agencies, culminating in at least one year in police work and afterwards, time spent in the *Allgemeine-SS* (the General SS), regarded as the core of the whole police organisation. On the way, recruits would be trained in leadership, with particular emphasis on what Himmler called the 'most significant thought in leadership training': how to win and retain the loyalty of subordinates.

Even before this, there had been a certain amount of crossover service between the Hitler Youth and the SS. It was open to SS personnel to become part-time leaders in the Hitler Youth and the SS had also provided several sports coaches to train Youth members. After June 1936, by order of the SSVT inspector, Paul Hausser, general training in the Hitler Youth became similar to that in the

Above: Gymnastics and athletics were meant to train the eye, improve physical control and heighten the fearlessness required of the Hitler Youth.

Allgemeine-SS. Former Youth leaders serving in the SSVT, like those serving in the army, were allowed to attend Hitler Youth camps and leadership courses. The RJF helped the SS–Hitler Youth marriage along by reducing the height requirements for those candidates who had not yet grown quite tall enough to qualify.

SS need for manpower

To an extent, this semi-merging of the two services was used by SS leaders who wanted to move in and exert their own influence on the Hitler Youth. However, the main motivation was the need for extra manpower and youth-power in particular. In 1936, the SSVT was relatively small, at only 9000 men, and

Above: A break for a bit of fun. In this picture, taken in May 1938, a Hitler Youth allows himself to be lathered and shaved by his companions.

although some 1400 Hitler Youth volunteers came forward after a recruiting drive masterminded by August Heissmeyer, only 800 proved to be suitable. Suitability depended heavily on proof of pure Aryan ancestry and even where this was forthcoming, it appears to have taken a long time for the evidence to be amassed. At Himmler's suggestion, Hitler Youth candidates were advised to start their research at least a year before seeking admission to the SS. Behind the scenes, however, the SS had been filching 17-year-olds from the Hitler Youth, so that the proofs required were inevitably patchy.

Qualifying for the SS

In all, qualifying to join the SS required the highest possible standards which only the *crème-de-la-crème* were able to meet. As well

as being perfect on ethnic, physical, racial, ideological and spiritual grounds, they also had to be temperamentally suited to soldiering. A detailed personal history had to be provided, together with good conduct certificates from the police. However, Himmler's original requirement that Aryan ancestry had to be proven back to the year 1650 was quickly changed, chiefly due to the colossal amount of genealogical investigation involved. One year of research before applying to the SS was not sufficient, even allowing for the fact that candidates were capable of sorting their way through a mass of church, community or family records. Due to Himmler's urgent need for new manpower, the date was therefore brought forward, first of all to 1800, and then to 1885, or a span of only two generations. As Himmler must have known, two 'pure' generations offered no real proof of a candidate's non-Jewish ancestry. Despite years of virulent anti-semitism in Germany, Jews were quite well assimilated into the general population, both socially and professionally, and intermarriage with non-Jews had been quite common for many years.

Time running out

By 1935 and 1936, Nazi Germany was starting to run short of time for preparing the Hitler Youth, the SS, and its other forces to establish the 'Thousand Year Reich'. By this stage, Hitler was knowingly taking international risks and ruffling the surface of the status quo established at the end of World War I. The Nazis had used their first three years in office to tighten their grip on Germany, clear out communists, socialists, trades unionists and other political enemies, build up their finances, consolidate their industries – especially the armaments industry – and prepare their assault on Jews and the equally 'inferior' gypsies. Now, however, they were coming out of the closet which had concealed their real intentions and proclaiming their agenda openly.

Hitler's announcement in March 1935 that the Third Reich was re-arming, followed by his formal repudiation of the Treaty of Versailles, had simply been preliminary manoeuvres. In September of the same year, the Nazis took the first legal moves against the Jews when the Nuremberg Laws stripped them of their citizenship and isolated them from political, professional and social life. Next, in October, Germany withdrew from the League of Nations. The international response was feeble. Politicians in Britain and France turned to appeasement, and there was no action from the League of Nations.

International protests

In January 1936, protests from the League of Nations at the treatment of the Jews received a stony rebuff from Hitler. By now, he was feeling bold enough to make a provocative statement, given in an interview with the French newspaper *France-Soir*, that he intended to recover Germany's lost colonies in Africa and the Pacific. On 7 March 1936, German forces re-occupied the Rhineland which had been demilitarised under the Treaty of Versailles. This, as Hitler announced to the Reichstag, was done on his personal orders. The German High Command had not approved, and the War Minister, General Werner von Blomberg, instructed that the troops should be withdrawn at once if France or Britain showed the slightest signs of armed retaliation.

There was no retaliation. Instead, the French were held back by the British, who placed their faith in Hitler's offer of a new treaty guaranteeing peace for the next 25 years. Three weeks after this, a plebiscite in Germany gave Hitler a 99 per cent approval rating. In April, those who did not vote lost their jobs. In September, the Wehrmacht began its most extensive manoeuvres since 1914, and in November, Germany concluded treaties with two other powers, Italy and Japan, whose own aggressions and posture had roused international concern.

Growing concern

In Britain, despite appeasement, the danger Nazi Germany presented was being recognised as something much more serious than mere sabre-rattling. Hitler was astute enough not to count on France and Britain remaining supine in the face of his muscular foreign policy. The Wehrmacht's reservations went further than worry over adverse consequences in the Rhineland: they feared the might of the French army in a future war and were daunted by the formidable barrier of the Maginot Line, built between 1929 and 1934, even though it ended at the frontier between France and Belgium. Beyond that, the forested Ardennes plateau, at its maximum height over 670m and – at that time – considered impossible for an army to traverse, ran towards the Channel coast.

There was, therefore, a strong ingredient of bluff and bluster in Hitler's posturings and the defiant face Nazi Germany showed the world at this time. As far as the Hitler Youth were concerned, the uncertainties of the mid-1930s transformed them from potential warriors into young men who might soon see real battle. From 1937, the paramilitary side of their training became their principal occupation.